MILLION MADE EASY

CORNELIUS FAIRWAY

Copyright © 2018 CORNELIUS FAIRWAY

All rights reserved.

ISBN-10: 172039122X
ISBN-13: 978-1720391227

DEDICATION

To My Readers
I hope that with luck, time, and the right application of these ideas, you will find fortune.

CONTENTS

	Introduction	i
1	The Product	1
2	The Audience	7
3	The Delivery	13
4	Unspoken Truth	19

INTRODUCTION

I cannot be the only person who has watched idiots become millionaires and thought, "Where is my million bucks?" I see it all the time on social media or the news where some punk teenager becomes filthy rich with little effort. I do not say this to discredit these individuals. They clearly had something figured out that I did not. However it got me thinking… Where will any of these "quick million" people be in a year or so when they blow it all. Then I realized that one million dollars isn't all that much any more. Spend some time researching it and you can find a lot of cases where someone has made and lost a million dollars or some other great some of money in an astonishingly short period of time.

Losing one million dollars is the easy part. I can easily write a five item list of things I would buy that could total up to a million bucks, and to many people out there it wouldn't even seem that extravagant. It is earning the one million dollars seems to be the hard part. To try to get you in the right mindset for this guide I urge you to shrink the idea of $1,000,000. It seems like such a distant goal or an abstract idea sometimes. Don't get caught up in calculating the hours of work, extra college degrees, years of investing, or any other quantifier people want to place on what it takes to make that money. This guide isn't directly about getting a successful career, investing tips, or any other specific method of making your money. This guidance is simpler and attempts to cover the broader ideas behind making your first million.

If you are looking for a step by step guide through life and "making your money work for you" then I suggest you find a financial advisor, because this is about MAKING the million. This is not about saving a million dollars, or having a million dollars after expenses. The goal is to help you turn an idea into money. In order for this to work you are going to need a practical understanding of life, or at least life as it applies to you and maybe people like you. Practical understanding is going to be a key theme here. What do people want or need, who are these people, how do these people communicate or interact with the world? Questions such as these, as well as your understanding of them, will severely impact your ability to make money with whatever you are offering.

With that we get into the three key ideas from which the rest of the book is derived from.

Idea One: What is your product or service? You will

need an original or at least mostly original product or service to sell, otherwise it is probably illegal in some way.

Idea Two: Who is your target audience? You are going to need people to buy your product or service in order for you to make money, so who are these people, and are there enough of them t make you the kind of money you want?

Idea Three: How are you going to get these people to your product? In order for your product to make money, your audience needs to know it exists and have a way to purchase it.

Now before we get started, I have just a couple of disclaimers. In no way is this a guarantee that you will make one million dollars. I do not promise you money. I am simply trying to guide you and provide direction for you to make your own money. Also, I am not saying that you will make one million dollars in any specific time frame. Lastly, I use a lot of ambiguity and generalities in this book. We live in a pretty litigious society, so I use this ambiguity and generality to avoid people who are a bit too opportunistic for my taste.

1 THE PRODUCT

-Everyone Has Something To Offer

    I am an optimist, so I like to think that everyone has something about them that is in some way original. I refuse to believe that any two people are entirely the same in how they think and engage with the world around them. There are certainly people who are similar, which leads to friends or couples completing each other's sentences and what not, but I don't believe that makes them entirely the same. So to me, that means that everyone has at least one thing to offer the world that is in some way different than everyone else. In those differences we attempt to derive our original product or service.

-Don't Make Someone Else's Money As Your Own

Lets take a quick look at the "original" part of our product or service. Yes your product must be your own, for the most part. The person who deiced that musical notes will be written the way they are doesn't sue everyone else who writes music. The inventor of the wheel doesn't fine every tire manufacturer. These are overly simplified examples, but you should be able to see the core principle there. Whatever your product is, make sure you are not crossing any legal boundaries. Check patents, copyrights, licensing, and so on as it pertains to what you are offering to ensure that your million dollars doesn't quickly get taken away from you in the courtroom. Consider all legal implications for your product or service. If your new and original idea is the resale of other people's products, the use and compilation of other people's talents, or in any way needs to provide credit to other people's efforts then you need to ensure that your are legally covered.

-Don't Spend A Dollar To Make Fifty Cents

Is your product cost effective? This is a very important question. If it takes $5.00 to make a product that people will only pay $4.00 for then you either need to rethink your manufacturing or pick a new product. This applies to the service industry as well. If you want to open a new restaurant, be sure that your sales are going to cover your operating expenses. This seems obvious, but this concept can easily get overlooked in the excitement of a new business prospect. Your bottom line will read as it reads. You can put all of the heart you want into your product but if its sale value isn't more than the cost to make it then you are losing money... The muffins may be made with love for $5 but that doesn't make it a $10 muffin. So be sure that you are not the only person who values your product above the manufacturing price, the customer needs to as well.

-Same Thing But Better

Understand the industry you are trying to enter into with your product or service. If you are making a functionally equal product as another company is and it doesn't conflict with any laws (i.e. patent or copyright law), then where is the appeal that you will require in order to compete with the other manufacturers? If you can make the "same product" at a lower manufacturing cost, then there is your competitive edge that will get you your sales. If you have access to better materials than your competitor does and can manufacture the product at the same cost, then that is where your competitive edge is found. As long as you keep the legal implications in mind, then your "original product/ service" doesn't need to be all that original. It can be the same thing, just better.

-Value Your Money, Not Your Product

This section may be a bit discouraging, and if you don't like it then I encourage you to ignore it. The concept is that if you can functionally make say $10 an hour by selling your product or service, but there is a job around the corner that is equally time demanding but pays $20 an hour…take the job. I am not a big fan of this idea because I firmly believe in being your own boss, following your own dreams and not someone else's, and valuing pride over money. However, if the goal is to make a million dollars, then you may have to sacrifice your original product or service if in the end it won't let you reach your goal in a satisfactory time period. There is a lot to be considered in a situation like this though and it is important to take into account all of the contributing factors. As stated before, do you want to be your own boss or would you rather make a bit more money and work for someone else? Calling the shots for your own product or service puts your success or failure on you. If you go work for someone then it becomes much easier to shift or share the blame of a failure for someone else's product or service that you were not all that emotionally invested in. That brings us to the topic of emotional investment. Personally, I am much more motivated to give my 100% in my own product than in someone else's. Someone else's product doesn't reflect who I am. Surely my work effort will reflect who I am, but only my own product could really show my originality, ingenuity, or personality. So ultimately you need factor your pride into your desire for your million bucks and when you hope to reach that goal.

-Today's, Tomorrow's, Or Yesterday's Product

Ensure your product is relevant. I could end this section right there with that first sentence, but I am going to go a little further into detail just to cover my bases. If you have a great idea on how to make music downloadable from the internet and store it on a portable device that can fits in your pocket then I think you may be to late. Conversely, if you are aspiring to be a fashion designer but your new trend won't catch on until you are dead then your product may be too early. Just look at any painter whose work wasn't valuable until after they died. Do your best to be sure that your product is today's product. There is certainly a little leeway with this concept though. Most people wouldn't have guessed that record players would make a comeback in the 2010's but sure enough they did, and of course no progress would be made if we didn't have innovators constantly working on the next big thing. The point is, there is more room for success with "today's" product than there is with a product too outdated or too futuristic. Hard to believe that a product too futuristic could be a bad thing, but if you brought a modern car too far into the past then you might just have gotten burned for witchcraft.

2 THE AUDIENCE

-Know Yourself

I am not trying to be philosophical or anything here. This certainly isn't a religious book, or guide for meditation. What I am saying here is that there was probably something in your life that lead you to creating your product or service, or maybe something that has drawn you to it. So whoever will be buying your product or service most likely has some sort of similarity with you. This is not a guarantee of course. Maybe you just had a great idea and know who would pay for it. However, even if you feel that your product isn't related to your needs, maybe just spend some time thinking on how you could relate to the people who will be buying it. You may come across some insight you weren't expecting.

-People Spend Money

People spend money, it is what they do. In my case, it is probably what I do best. I am pretty good at spending money, then at the end of the month I look at my accounts and ask, "where did it all go?" There are a lot of people in America. There are a lot of people in the world, and basically all of these people are spending money in some way or another. I mean really think about how much money there is in the world. A definite answer is probably only one internet search away. These people are constantly spending their money on this thingy or that whatever, and how many of those thingies or whatevers aren't actual necessities? There is plenty of "disposable" income getting moved around out there. With all of that cash moving around all of the time, why can't just a million bucks of it be spent on your product or service? Whether your product is life saving, a daily essential, a luxury item, or just simply a fun item, there certainly must be enough disposable income out there for someone to buy it.

-Enough People In Your Audience

The next question you should be asking yourself is concerning the amount of people willing to buy your product. Are there going to be enough people who want to buy your product in order for you to make your one million dollars? A simple equation that I am not going to spell out for you should make it obvious as to how many people need to buy your product in order for you to make your desired amount of money. It is going to involve your expected sales price, total expenses per product or service, and probably a few other variables depending on the industry your particular product or service falls into. Whatever the total number of people you come up with should represent how many people that will need to purchase your product in order for you to make your desired amount of money. I will now refer to that group as your audience. Your audience doesn't need to be a specific number and certainly don't let this number limit you. Of course your goal should be to sell your product or service to as many people as possible, but it is helpful to have an idea of your target audience's size.

-Know Your People

You will need a thorough understanding of who your audience is in order to maximize your effectiveness in getting them to purchase your product or service. We are going to get into a lot of who your audience is in the next few sections. The types of questions you should keep in mind are things like: how does my audience think, how do they communicate, where are they located, what makes them similar, what makes them different, how do they spend their time, are they an exclusive group or inclusive? The more in depth you get to know your target audience, the more successful you will be in selling them your product or service.

-Audience Location

The physical location of your audience is going to play a role in your success. Not only in marketing your product or service, but in its functionality and survivability. If your product is intended for college students on spring break, then you may notice that the hit spring break location moves every couple of years, that is a nomadic audience in a way. However, if your audience is the "stay at home moms" then that audience probably sticks to a solid routine the majority of the time. Your audience's physical location helps define who they are. It could be regional such as nation, state, or continent. It could be much smaller than that such as what stores your audience frequents the most: coffee shops, grocery stores, or sporting good stores. Don't expect to make your million selling surfboards in Nebraska or selling snow shoes in Hawaii.

-Audience's Time

How does your audience spend their time? Parents nowadays would probably tell you that their children spend most of their time on the internet. Some people prefer to spend their leisure time in the outdoors. Workaholics of course spend most of their time working. Take a minute and think where you spend most of your time. Do you go into somewhat of a different mental state depending on where you are and how your time is being spent? If I am in a meeting and bored out of my mind then I immediately start looking for a distraction. I spend a lot of time commuting to and from work, but I go completely blank during that drive and couldn't tell you what song came on the radio. How is your audience spending their time and what is their mind doing during that time? Where is their focus? Just because they spend a lot of time on one particular event doesn't mean that that is the best time for your product to reach them. Look at how they spend their time and how they actually value their time.

-Audience Communication

I am not going to spend a lot of time in this section because I will get more into it in chapter three, but think on how your audience communicates. Do they talk over social media, email, phone, letters, in person? What language do they use? Obviously you need to know their actual language (i.e. English French, Spanish etc.), but do they curse, is there a local accent or dialect they may respond better or worse to? During my time in the military I had a superior who would say, "if you aren't cursing then your aren't really communicating."

-Inclusive Or Exclusive

You will need to be especially careful with this idea if your expected audience size is right at the amount of money you hope to make with your product. Is your audience inclusive or are they exclusive? There are those groups of people who increase the value of a product or service based on how many people cannot or do not have it. If that is the case then ensure your audience size and price of your product or service will achieve your profit goals. The inclusive audience is probably the more growth market. When the success of your product with your intended audience causes more people to purchase it than you may have originally anticipated you get what I call an inclusive audience. There are pros and cons to both kinds of audience, the exclusive and inclusive alike. The exclusive audience are more likely to spend more money on a product due to its exclusivity, but an inclusive audience is more likely to expand your audience. This is going to get addressed a little more in chapter three.

3 THE DELIVERY

-You Care The Most

You are going to be hard pressed to find someone to sell your product who cares as much as you do. Sure there are marketing agencies and what not, but they are paid to care about your product or service. The person who has put the most time into it is you. You should be the most effective salesperson on your team. You probably know your product better than anyone and could describe it with more heart than anyone else you can find. I am not saying that outside expertise isn't warranted. You may not be a great salesman, but you should be hands on with whoever is getting your product or service into the hands of the customer. Together with whoever you are trusting with your marketing/distribution/sales will develop a plan, but they will need your view of the product to influence their actions. You need to be the one who cares the most about your product's success the most.

-Inclusive Branding

This was touched on earlier in chapter two. Inclusive branding is when your target audience as well as your product invite more people to buy your product or service. You can see a lot of success with this kind of branding when the latest trend comes out that originally makes no sense to some people, but then about a month later they are roped in with the crowd. I am a huge victim of this. I am always against the newest fashion trends and can typically hold out on buying into it for a month or two. Then I inevitably cave in and buy the new shoes or sunglasses or shorts or whatever it is that month. The products themselves are designed to make everyone the same basically. It is affordable to the masses and has wide appeal. In the services industry it can be a little different. A new hotel moved into my city and it seemed to have something for everyone. Fancy restaurants, affordable bars, a pool for the kids, large entertainment area suited for just about everyone, spa, and the list goes on. Room prices to fit a variety of budgets, but generally affordable. The goal for the place was to meet everyone's needs but maintain the different environments that different customers may be used to. They succeeded in inclusive branding.

-Exclusive Branding

Do not get caught up on the word "exclusive" or mistake it for pretentious. We have all seen those brands out there that expensive for no real reason. The product quality is okay, and yet the price is insane. That is where I would start to use the word pretentious, but then again I respect their branding because it is working for them. I prefer to look at the products that are exclusive due to actual product value and specific target audiences. There is nothing wrong by my account with being in the private jet business, and naturally that is going to be a rather exclusive clientele due to the price range. So understand that there is a balance to be had somewhere in there, where you are trying to falsely brand something as exclusive rather than truly having an exclusive brand and audience. Don't try to oversell your product, but don't undersell it either. Know what your craftsmanship is worth.

-Free Marketing

People are going to see that word "free" above and get pretty excited. That reaction is appropriate. Everybody loves free, but it usually comes with a catch. The catch this time is how much work you have to put into getting to the "free marketing point". Word of mouth is the best marketing tool because once it starts then it is often a snow ball effect and just keeps rolling and getting bigger. You get the first sale to one person, then they talk to their friends who talk to their friends and so on… It can be counter productive as well because if that first sale goes poorly, that snowball can often grow faster. In high school if you told a friend that you got an "A" on a test, that news would probably die right there. When you tell that same friend who you kissed under the bleachers…that news spreads pretty fast. Depending on the industry your product or service fall within will dictate which high school scenario your word of mouth marketing takes. People are more likely to talk about what new restaurant has incredible food as opposed to what facial tissue is the softest, but if that facial tissue causes a burning rash… that news will probably spread pretty fast. Different industries can have very different snowballing patterns.

-Not Free Marketing

This is pretty obvious. Not free marketing is marketing that you pay for. There are so many options here. Radio, TV, newspaper, internet marketing, door to door salesmen, and pretty much countless other avenues of marketing your can choose from. You could avoid this and do your marketing directly by starting up that free marketing by yourself and trying to sell your product or service directly but that can be an incredibly difficult and slow way to get started. With social media you can certainly get that ball rolling quicker but in most cases may just be easier to hire a professional. Your marketing and sales growth will most likely go hand in hand. This is because as you sell more of your product you can afford a more comprehensive marketing approach and you will need a more comprehensive marketing approach because you have already sold your product or service to those who have received your current marketing scheme. This is a very broad stroke at marketing a product, not all products or services fall within this example.

-Distribution

Distribution can be a road block for some people. How do you physically get your product or service to your customer? As it has been in this whole book, this will vary greatly depending on the particular industry your product or service pertains to. Consider the logistics alone of starting a company with a physical product that people buy online. Will you be able to manage the packaging and shipping of your inventory to all of your customers? If so then that is fantastic, if not then you get into the logistics of it all. Do you plan on selling your product through another retailer? Does the service you provide require another medium such as transportation or vendor support? The costs can really start to pile up if your service or product require extensive logistical support.

-Tying Two And Three

This last section is just to tidy up some obvious but loose ends. In case there is a gap that needs filling in for better comprehension of chapters two and three. Getting your audience and your product together. A simple way to view it and then extrapolate a more appropriate application for your product or service is this; what social media application does your target audience use? Post on and connect with as many people as you can and let the internet take it from there. Get the word out in any and every way that you can, try to let your audience do the rest.

4 UNSPOKEN TRUTH

-Going To Need Some Luck

Unfortunately there will always be some luck involved. You can put in a lot of planning and think of very possible contingency you may need, but sometimes in life you may just need some luck. Maybe the market isn't right for your product. Maybe someone somewhere else beat you by just one day. I wish it weren't true, but luck does play a factor.

Your Product:

_____
_____
_____
_____
_____
_____

Your Audience:

_____
_____
_____
_____
_____
_____

Your Delivery:

_____
_____
_____
_____
_____
_____

www.ingramcontent.com/pod-product-compliance
Lightning Source LLC
Chambersburg PA
CBHW030045230526
45472CB00005B/1690